DEVIANT

"In *Deviant*, Patrick Grace calls out from the charged and sometimes lonely terrain of queer male intimacy. In brilliant and emotionally devastating work, Grace reminds us how the hunger for connection and the desire for lasting redemption unites us in our longing. *Deviant* is a collection to savour, introducing a brave new voice in Canadian poetry."

—**TREVOR CORKUM**, author of *The World After Us*

"Imagine a poem as a traffic light, blinking 'stop, go, and wait.' In the hands of Patrick Grace, a phrasemaker of immense skill, these states are combined and recombined to form a highway to the living, breathing world. *Deviant* is the best kind of poetic debut—written to stand out, and in doing so subverting all expectation."

—**JIM JOHNSTONE**, author of *The King of Terrors*

"*Deviant* deftly and with heartbreaking tenderness explores the beauty, yearning, grief, and boundless cycles of discovery involved in queer realization. With a narrative poise that invites the reader in as an intimate witness, Patrick Grace lays down a mosaic of moments that capture the wonders and cruelties of queer being, from heat-warped summer days to coiling truck exhaust and late urban nights. Grace's poetry is a gift—at once confessional and intimate, yet allowing the queer reader to find themselves time and again within the verse. *Deviant* is an earnest testament to the way a life unfolds in the face of societal rigidities, told with a voice that carries a mesmerizing composure, yet which surges with the undercurrents of a fierce and luminous poetic grace."

—**RHIANNON NG CHENG HIN**, author of *Fire Cider Rain*

"*Deviant* deftly embodies that complex space of queer selfhood and interaction and longing. What a journey, what a joy to move through its beautiful, bruising language, its resonance, and all the ways it makes hope and hurt alike sing."

—**DOMINIK PARISIEN**, author of *Side Effects May Include Strangers*

"The glinting and sensually rich poems in Grace's *Deviant* are in possession of such a harrowing nostalgia. Tread carefully, but tread nonetheless."

—**JOHN ELIZABETH STINTZI**, author of *Junebat*

DEVIANT

POEMS

PATRICK GRACE

UNIVERSITY of ALBERTA PRESS

Published by

University of Alberta Press
1-16 Rutherford Library South
11204 89 Avenue NW
Edmonton, Alberta, Canada T6G 2J4
amiskwaciwâskahikan | Treaty 6 |
Métis Territory
uap.ualberta.ca | uapress@ualberta.ca

LIBRARY AND ARCHIVES CANADA CATALOGUING IN PUBLICATION

Title: Deviant / Patrick Grace.
Names: Grace, Patrick, author.
Series: Robert Kroetsch series.
Description: Series statement: Robert Kroetsch series | Poems.
Identifiers:
Canadiana (print) 20230551637 |
Canadiana (ebook) 20230551645 |
ISBN 9781772127416 (softcover) |
ISBN 9781772127621 (EPUB) |
ISBN 9781772127638 (PDF)
Subjects: LCGFT: Poetry.
Classification: LCC PS8613.R3329 D49 2024 | DDC C811/.6—dc23

First edition, first printing, 2024.
First printed and bound in Canada by Houghton Boston Printers, Saskatoon, Saskatchewan.
Editing by Annick MacAskill.
Proofreading by Mary Lou Roy.

A volume in the Robert Kroetsch Series.

University of Alberta Press is committed to protecting our natural environment. As part of our efforts, this book is printed on Enviro Paper: it contains 100% post-consumer recycled fibres and is acid- and chlorine-free.

University of Alberta Press gratefully acknowledges the support received for its publishing program from the Government of Canada, the Canada Council for the Arts, and the Government of Alberta through the Alberta Media Fund.

Canada | Canada Council for the Arts | Conseil des Arts du Canada

Alberta Government

CONTENTS

Men of the outer world dash me to bits.

ELIZABETH WILLIS
"The Human Abstract"

I

II

III

IV

V

WHY NOT

It began in a field where two boys
played in a circle of melting snow.

Creeping phlox flourished,
lights dotted the hills,

and the finches and foxes
followed the melt to the river

while the rest of the world
pressed buttons and touched screens.

Budding bluebells lined a sodden sheen
where the boys found a worn-out baseball.

They hurled it back and forth, imitating
dads and uncles and older brothers—

overhand throw, pro-pitcher wannabes
aiming dead centre at the ribs.

The younger slugger stumbled on a catch
and landed face-first in frost. Little

leaguer. An echo struck inside him.
He packed the ball in fistfuls of snow

and flung it back, bullseye to the face,
the eyes. He did as he was taught by men—

why not? No one was watching,
and boys learn the edges

of what they hold in their hands
when angered.

DASTARDLY

Dastardly, you heard it right
from Mom in the front seat,
fuel pump on the fritz
again, old Volvo slowing the hill,
the word like another you know
off TV and thriller movies
when the good guy gets foiled,
as it happens, a minor setback,
the kid high in a black walnut tree
across the street, just a boy really,
about your age and shaking
out the shells, *that little shit,*
rolling them into the road
to catch under hot tires
and catching your eye
in the backseat, giving you
a onceover, the middle finger,
innuendo blooming at the mouth,
devilish boy in red shorts
shaking something large and young
inside you to break it open.

NICK THE DICK

As a kid I could be witty and tragic all at once,
chasing the boys in the lower field and screaming

Nick the dick to the one I loved most.
As in, planting his fist under my ribs.

As in, this is what I am:
a boy who cries after a hug.

You better let him go. He feels too much.
Architect of my body, I am no longer there.

No boy ever is. I imagined his kisses soft,
fists raining down after a soccer match.

Fuck I could run back then. So could he.
The best intentions run through me.

Our gym teacher called us bellicose,
as in, I taunted and Nick came

to pin me down, that childish expression
of rancour stinging me to the ground.

I begged for the repetition.
I kept his face close to mine.

As in, his class photo swiped and squirrelled
under my foam mattress, revisiting the fold

night after night like a bad dream.
My breath broke splendidly. I slept on my hands.

Years later I swap stillness for internet streams.
I fall in love with moving pictures.

Nick is married now. A beautiful Greek wedding,
crowns of orange blossoms looping on his Instagram profile.

My friend request is still pending. Please follow me
back. What makes you think you didn't like to chase?

I begged for the repetition, held on to what I could,
puppeteering his grade-school gym socks.

My guidance counsellor said I had room
to improve. Potential. He called me

bright. I am anything but a light,
diving out of myself

and laddering into the sky.

THE FIRST

Simple, really, heralding the first
day of summer vacation in the early
hours, cartoons on mute,

the overhead vacuum hum
collecting our lost pieces,
loud sensations down

the street like construction
or a blur of men punching
holes in each other.

Either way, something built
and torn apart again.
My low window is a flood

risk in heavy rainfall. Double
pane glass on backorder.
The man next door

stands at the mirror—
he dries off behind the blinds
with a thick white towel

and does to himself the hurt
that I do to myself, too. Watching him
I know the word

for what I am:
Power Ranger,
naked troll

lost in the heating vent,
but I don't say these words
when I kneel

next to my bed
and think of him,
the lights I touch.

A CONE OF LIGHT

On my bare stomach I disappeared
old toys down crumbling holes in the porch.
The kids next door soared on a new swingset, *clink clink*
over the fence hidden in rhododendrons,
birds chattering, Mom asleep again somewhere.
My sister ran barefoot along the burning
sidewalk, gate open—they all swung
to the *clink clink* of the chain links.
I wasn't allowed over. Nothing
new, breaking heads off trolls
with bejewelled bellies
and disappearing them down the hole.
After the last beheading
I stretched myself on the sidewalk
and burned ants with my magnifying glass.
I was still learning
about convex lenses in school.
A cone of light entered my palm.
Nothing. A screen door banged
and the mother screamed
for her children, calling them back
or calling them away.
It might've been lunchtime. The sun was high,
our mom asleep somewhere,
traffic and chittering and grass
upon grass upon grass.

WATERGUN

The school day ended we rushed back
in the blistering heat—

Green hose running down the side of his house—

Minivan still gone from the driveway—

First, at the mouth,
he knew his name by the shape of my mouth—

My brother still asks about the waterguns
I borrowed that day—

A warm likeness spread between us—

We called it *spillage*
and waterblasted the gravel—

Time a bulletblur
those final days
of June—

Licorice root on our breath—

Two boys reflected in a basement window—

Peeling paint crumbled against my face,
blood in the tooth—

My body glass under the eavestrough—

The sun burned its gold coin—

Minutes later they came back,
gravel popping under hot tires—

RAVINE

My body was a needle
in the ravine—easily lost and forgotten

where spume and shade met the tunnel's metal grate.

Making my peace by the painted brick wall, I screamed
at the noise of boys and soccer balls

crashing on the other side,

late for practice, a river of rust running

through my mind.

The community centre entrance
led to a library and a pool and a gym.

Mom dropped me off out front at 9am

in our dying Honda—

Hey hun, have fun

Before cell phones, men hung around

to watch and wait for the moment
a mother's eyes turned away—

the gold hardened in my gut—

I followed him down
to the ravine where signs warned of lines

lain underground

be wary of digging
where live wires may lie

sleepless at the tunnel mouth
and taking what the light offered

TRAFFIC LIGHT

I remember the night my brother came home
dragging a stolen traffic light like a body. Late fall
and my legs dangled out the bedroom window,
heavy rain sailing down, the sound like pennies
on the corrugated shingles. He'd snuck out again, disappearing
over the eavestrough in jeans and a black hoodie.
Videogame gunfire popped on repeat under his door.
Those days he memorized monologues
in his room and spoke them to the wall, the campfire
scene from *The Revenant*, finding God in a squirrel.
I tried the book but gave up, as often as we did
in that house. Our lives yielded to the yellow.
Mom fell asleep before dark under the rhododendrons.
The familiar: the back gate and its broken wheel,
the trample of my brother's boots, cigarette in his lips,
that singular burning eye. Sweet clove smoke.
He pulled the light behind him with one hand,
overgrown grass flattening under the weight.
I waited for the back door, the inevitable grunt.
This one weighed heavy on him for years
and for years after he never gave up
where he found it, three lights burning
across his walls in blinks of stop, go, wait.

NIGHTCALL

Every night a distant railsqueal cut through me,
my room full of broken yellow trains.
I was still a boy with boyhood dreams,

wandering up the hill from Kits Beach
in hot pink shorts, legs gleaming
banana-scented sunscreen sheen, ready

to run with trains along the Arbutus track.
My mom and sisters dove into the sand.
Are you listening? I was still a boy.

Two older kids banged rocks along the steel lines
and came at me all bearhug and roughdown.
Blundersight. I landed eye to eye with a railspike.

Years later Vancouver would rip out
the tracks and replace them with bike lanes.
One kid treaded my spine in soccer cleats

while the other tousled my hair
like a playful lover. Every night I waited
for the sound to rouse me from a dream,

the whistle, the groan, the backspray
of pebbles and oil, how dark the gap
between the cars, learning to taste

another boy's spit and dreaming
it could be warm, secreted
special, just for my mouth.

I

II

III

IV

V

LAYOVER

Descend. Here's a crowd that's reached the end
of metal body scans. And here's this guy
among the cougars, the business cubs:
his eyes are blue, they catch my own, I ask
to sit, he says, *Sure man, I'm Bjorn from Iceland,*
and clasps a thick, rough hand in mine. Smooth jaw,
clipped accent. Something gives inside: I want
the two of us to sample berry wine
in bed. O imagination, how you twist
man's apprehension! But shit, I'm not like that.
Not like that sleaze by the bar, his hands on her
skirt. Been a rough afternoon. Another order's up.
Me and Bjorn watch the world side by side.
We shoot the shit: the Habs, a naked infant's
teeth around a mother's nipple, anything
to stop my open hands. The walls are glass.
We watch the sky, the way it falls, plane
propellers trimming bird wings. Bone-dull thump—
the waitress coldcocks the sleazy man. No one
gets involved. There's a voice in the walls
and it calls out a name. *That's me,* says Bjorn.
The sun breaks through the glass. He takes his leave
in dusted jeans, my head a bloody mess
like the sleaze on the floor by the bar, hands open.

STRAWBERRY ISLAND

We named our world for strawberries
but none grew that summer among the bog rot

and licorice root. We lifted deadfall into a makeshift
lean-to and wound our trouble through sword ferns,

samara seeds wizened with time.
A purple fog rose over the lagoon.

Somewhere under the thickened brush, a thrust
as a varied thrush scooted for cover, the hills

silvering at nightfall. Our language lingered
illicit. He was a boy pushing me

down with shimmering hands,
a face that intimated a fox jowl.

Nettle breath. I was a boy
and I was lying with another boy,

terror's first pinch at my hamstrings,
wolf in my throat and leaping.

ARTHUR

I have the best memory
of what it means
to be gay
at the end
of summer.
By gay I mean
wondrous,
the sun
hitting
our thankless bodies
on an Okanagan
lakeside dock.
Wasps warmed
to the cedarwood.
We were equal
parts
queer and water,
loosening canoe ropes
off their cleats,
hands full
of boyish desire
in the late air.
The other kids
in the valley
mastered archery lessons
across the lake.
I slipped your shirt off.
Kokanee salmon
disturbed the water's surface.
Somewhere
a voice yelled
bullseye,
the word
lifting across
the volcanic cliff
face.

TEARDOWN

I want you to tell me about your side of town,
edge of the crumbling bridge I phantom to
in backseats on school days, passing through

on my knees and never existing, never
spending the night, maw ripe and agape,
nearing the water outside a glass tower,

chandelier above the river lit and spinning.
I want you to tell me about your place,
parts of a whole aglow in voice-activated shades

of winter blue and spearmint green,
ghosts of plum and red mulberry.
Your night-time self is lighthearted,

silly, cupping water in the shower
and watching it fall after we fuck.
Of all your selves I hate the early riser

the most, determined with coffee
and postdoctoral notes for the day.
Your phone screen lights up early.

Potential hookups text you. You find time
to drive across town most evenings.
The train is on time this morning and I feel lucky.

A single cop car stops to investigate
vandalized artwork across the boulevard.
Sometime in the night the word TEARDOWN

appeared where splashes of pink and yellow and sky
blue intersect. A gold plaque reads *fingerpaint*.
It's often here I wander when I leave you

long before the world begins to stir.
Somewhere in the hemorrhage of colour
floats a man on a metal beam

wielding his tools and solvent,
never quite smoothing the glass
to how it glowed before.

STUDENT DEBT

Lately I've been returning before sundown
or after hours, between split shifts dishing out

greasebowl eggs and styrofoam coffee cups
at J's Breakfast World. Not that the brew's bad—

some nights it's the only way to stay awake
long enough to skim *The Unwritten Rules*

of PhD Research, long enough to survey bottleneck
truckers rolling in to unload

milk, bacon, house-brand pancake mixes,
one last stop before the interstate.

Full moon, they ease onto the steel flatbed
to smoke, crotches thrust at the sky.

My thesis confounds boundaries with personal space.
My tongue unfurls an outgoing lane of *hello*.

I proposition the short one around back
with a popped-fly blowjob, his skin thick

and brick coloured. My body must give
express consent. I straddle the line

between inexperienced and educated,
Gen-Y think tank chugging along. Late night

texts from Mom: *need money? coming home?*
Cross-country Greyhound tomorrow. Can't wait.

CATERPILLAR

More than anything, I wanted
to break in the new sofa, its body L-shaped
as a metamorphosizing caterpillar.
I positioned its lime-green contours
in the darkest corner of the room.
Scented candles released dragonfruit.
I anchored books in piles by the window,
ascending them like a paper staircase.
I was new to the city. A return
to adolescent solipsism, you could say.
I broke what bent first.
Does it come as a shock
that I engaged in light dusting
even at the knock,
rinsed with mouthwash,
let the wine touch open air,
forgot to tell a friend I was alone
as the stranger entered and locked the door.

THE DARK GAP

Years ago, the dark gap I imagined
wide enough to have forgotten
how it started in my childhood—

the oddities of men
in Eaton's catalogues, cutouts
of jeans and boots and tube socks
Christmas wish lists
full-colour inserts—

this one like my gym teacher,
this one like my bus driver.

A long time passed.
I managed to sleep.

Years later I tasted my adult
self in a sweet luminous blur
on my knees
in the back row, losing
a game meant for parties
of one or less.

My body is not incorruptible.
He reached inside me
for the last favours.
What vile goodbyes
waiting for it to pass.

IT'S LIKE THAT, IS IT

I come for the free coffee
but stay for the men committed
to the men committed to their wives.

It's simple, unsinging the ring
until she's pregnant with his kid.
I grew my hair to the shoulder bone

but not my breasts. I hacked off nothing.
I disintegrated in the mirror.
The steam pulled back to reveal

my never self, my never person.
Pour me another, I think
I'm just under the limit

to hold lightning in my veins.
The loneliest homos
are the ones I sing awake

when the rain asks
if they'll stay till late morning.
I'd like to tell him

this is the last time,
turning the same corner
of what could be versus what is.

THE CIRCUIT

You can't keep pretending all the time.
Men beckon you into the stall with a wave

and you joke about lowering yourself to their level
before getting on your knees. Get this—

the all-night circuit has room for two more.
As if you needed a reason to feign loneliness.

That's where it began, all night, doing the right things.
I am almost 19. The floor is gold, the machines click in.

What makes this the right age to die. That's all we want,
to be surrounded in a bed near an open window.

You are surrounded in a bed and open to new things.
My reticence holds me in the corner, counting

holes in the walls, the black pages I blew through
as a child, Lite-Brite pegs brightening a dinosaur mouth.

The ceiling is made of glass. Someone bursts a glitterbomb
and I'm blown forward in the crowd. I'm asking for it

to be daylight again so I can sleep without dreaming.
My fondest memories of you come when I wake alone,

dusting glitter off the bed for days afterward.
The party favours came in lovely colours.

I

II

III

IV

V

THE BIG DARK

Something big and dark has made its home
inside the wintered gas station out back. Did you
see? It entered city limits when you left
the funny pages for the dog to tear apart.

The school's been put on lockdown. At the creek
preteens build a three-tiered smoker's den
from vandalized debris. I've set alight
the hairspray from back then, small explosions,

rainbow-coloured flight. The big dark
has taken residence at Kingdom Hall.
The nonbelievers don't come back. Come back.
The town's gone

mad for baked beans and D-cell batteries
to power Geiger counters in its wake.
I wait in line with Bristol board and magic
markers. They say it's landed on the lake, its wings

propelling little hurricanes. How many times the word
"future" gets sucked under the checkout belt.
See what happens when they take our guns?
No animal lends muscle to intent.

When the town declares a state of emergency,
only the vulnerable remain. It's here, Magog.
I lift the interphone. The hunt begets the wait.
I've grown to miss the static and the fog.

SOMEDAY YOU WILL ACHE

Not every driver wanted me dead
that summer of broken yellow lights.

I played chicken on the highway and little
by little the stars sped up. The men slowed

down. I spread-eagled over the asphalt—
it was the warmest hug I'd ever felt.

It takes nineteen minutes to swap out a tire,
even less to ask forgiveness.

You can't tackle me if I'm already down.
Curb stomping creates the finest dance move.

Thunder spread its roots beneath my ear.
The water lowered a tunnel within me.

That day I was capable of many things:
seeing my breath in summer—flying, even,

or giving credence to a fresh roadkill,
the speed in which it left us. Every second

a new wheel of opportunity presented itself.
The curb reassured me things were looking up.

YOU LOOK OLDER

These aren't the words
I want to hear as he finds
his clothes. I'll admit,
it's been a few years
and I don't live here anymore.
The hotel walls are glass.
A billboard outside reads
day is for resting. Words like this
have aged the city.
We never stay in bed long.
Each time undoes
the newness
of the first,
hand in my mouth and climbing.

AFLOAT

In upstate New York, a man jumps fifty feet
from a common hackberry tree and survives.

He calls it floating, wheeled from the ER to neuropsych.
Years after you robbed me for a hit of smack

no one guessed we'd be cheek to cheek
in a speakeasy fronting as a witch league,

TVs blaring the man's failed suicide.
Something Wiccan This Way Comes borders the bar

but no one's done magic for months.
It's become a dive for upstate drivel.

Drunken morosis to meek meliorism.
Natural beauty drives away the best of us.

An easy split to the Adirondacks
if the snowdrifts don't kill you first.

You ask me to watch the bowl of peanuts
while you shoot up behind the bar.

Do you think you're happy?
Where will your body be

a year from now, washed up
with the black dogs on a spit of land.

Billy, it's gotta be your babyface
or your deep blues that keep me

from calling you out, that keep me
from calling the cops on the meth

you keep stashed in your pack.
What do I tell my mom when she asks

why you're back in town
or why it never worked out?

I knew you once, connecting with my jaw.
The plastic ravens balter overhead.

I'm handfuls into the peanuts when two men
disappear and return afloat, stricken, bloody,

a sudden hullabaloo in the street,
some quick and dangerous sound

like air released or a gust tearing east
and seizing with it the lightest of debris

but there's no wind tonight,
there's been no wind for days.

TOUCH ANYWHERE TO BEGIN

He's coming for the back of my throat,
a shard of paper bullets. I didn't ask for it.

The sky is made of gunmetal and sharp
nimble things. I catch what I can, count

full rotation to the next level. Are we there yet?
The overpass marks the last chicken exit.

Inevitable: removing the blind
when we get where we're going, where

the border guard will seize our phones and wallets.
My ID has expired. Is it still me? We plow west.

At the red light my body itches to jump and roll,
the truck smelling of sage and burnt

plastic. The sky reaches umber.
Someone's cast fire where it shouldn't be.

AS IF

As if the one-way drive after dark
because the return was never spoken.

As if the son who leaves his mother
the same way his father did.

As if The Wanderer bar
where men like you hide.

As if the fool on his seventh pour
and the fooled on his eighth.

As if the climb returns to knock
down the stairs in a knuckleball,

his hand at your teeth,
copper ring carrying a familiar scent

to bite down as if in a dance.
As if suddenly your body, your breath.

THE FLOOR WAS WATER

After the last public blowout in a doorway at the edge of Granville Island, I wandered west, far from the late-night comedy show. I wasn't laughing anymore. Light silvered the hill. I left him treading behind me under the bridge, his threats an echo, the concrete lending him its depth. I found an empty house and sat on the kitchen floor. I tugged a bag of ice from the freezer and cradled a few cubes in my hand. They numbed me. I traced the linoleum tiles, squared each one, and when the floor was water, I entered it. A dark thin pool. My eyes listened for the echo and I heard the bridge, the headless fire growing underneath.

THE GASLIGHTER

what I remember most / the yelling light / look left
look right / the man a curtain over / maybe drunk /
quoting self-delusions to the wall / say your name for
me / window / asphalt / you'll remember it wrong /
this brick is fiction and other detached logic / open
my mouth / the past swoops out / tell me your version /
a hurried thought / scuttle / knife lift it / how many
times / iterated on a scale of 1 to 10 / someone wheels
the curtain man away / they gave me all these tests /
my wristband a sign of willing participation / the blue
men have more questions / I can't count anyone out
but myself /

AS YOU WERE

Can you undo the threat
go back to the rock
sleeping under peat moss
everything in its place
my head blown away
the world moving through it

it's never the shape
of what you hold
that scares me, rather
the rubber band
bouncing back
sufficient, as you were

I wish you'd follow
up on that promise to break
every one
of my fingers
so I can point myself
in a new direction

SWITCHRAIL

at first the hollows I didn't recognize
bellclap told me nothing of the long hours

inside myself   the train
                                    coming   how bright

the flowers for his 30th bday
the long hallway   bao bei in chinatown

never been never
tried electrified eel / nettle

dumplings / wagyu from snake
river farms /

close to twenty friends invited   denied   only ten allowed

who has twenty
close friends   I mean real

close
when he shows you

        who he is, believe him
        inviting friends to sit on his lap   heady   heavy

        hands in their hair

                a little
                        kissy too   they all go for it his charm

I'm at the bottom
of my first drink at the end

of the table   elegant   local
distinct

        their words   flip over

to the back you'll find useful
phrases for social interaction—

It's not you

I'm not

You are

Do you have

a light? The switchrail

divides without echo How

do I say that?

I

II

III

IV

V

A VIOLENCE

in the dream he'd forgotten
the winded violence
the night the first
change the crumbling ceiling

all I saw was up
I forgave him for forgetting
the heady violence
the rowel, clumsy dance

around me still I go
and look what I find:

the cliché or the truth
the water or the truth
the bellclap or the dog bark
the hard fist or the harder word

can you describe a violence?
works a hotel desk does he
wears a smile for strangers does he
winds up drunk weekdays does he

around me still I hear
all it takes
a moment of courage
can you hold courage
wield courage
drink up courage
bite down courage
or is courage another one
of those things you say

when was the first
violence
man to man
did violence start slow
did violence build up
did violence lean down
or do the bending

who admitted it
first
was photography invented
was DNA a thing
fingerprinting   swabbing   uhlenhuth testing

did they believe you
did the man in blue believe
another man
committed the violence
because it's always a man
you have to talk to
on the other end
you have to convince
on the other end
who finds it
inconclusive
domestic
misunderstanding
I still find
glass in the bedroom
the yelling light
the breath over and over

HEATWAVE

How long ago was it, just last week
the streetlight burst again when I passed

underneath. I guessed coincidence
after the second time, remember,

when the heatwave shattered record-
store windows and the power

we all held in our hands extinguished
for a few minutes, and we crawled out,

begrudgingly, into wonder
of the faces around us.

It lasted a short time.
In faraway cities, trains changed tracks.

Birds alighted the switchrails.
North became east and the earth tilted.

It lasted a short time. The last time
the light burned out above me

on the road away from home,
my hands held nothing but glass.

Passing headlights cut the night.
My chances decreased the further I ran.

DOCUMENT

are you still scared
out of sight now
the evidence wet with air

recall it
in your own words
awake, briefly

the fire not yet headless
the turn of a lock
shaming my body

Do you feel
like you are in danger
I have never felt

so thin and so clear   speaking
Can you tell me your name
speaking   *Can you tell me*

What is your location   eyelevel with a mountain
Is the danger immediate
his fire grows an echo in the wall

hushed   swift
has he returned to repeat
or follow through

Do you know where
he is at this moment   *Are you*
afraid for your safety

911 who are you
here for   I am only
a feeling or reality

911 how do you
measure danger my panic
or your professional opinion

is this what you call
authentication
am I real part lightning now

am I only consequence
end result *I am only*
the dispatch I can only

take your information
address date of birth
take his information
address date of birth

Do you have a file number is it
consecutive seven digits long
whole parts of me
disrupted iterated in sequences of 1s and 0s

repeated
the attention unwanted
repeated and unwanted attention
who repeated the unwanted fear

the safety fear the solo fear
the repeated fear his drink
does he drink repeatedly does he unwant
what he wanted when his attention

repeats its soundless echo
hotel exit faster

parking lot faster
highway onramp faster   on foot   no shoulder

I entered the breath
the inside of a bell   leaden air
halved and unhinged
his pursuit an iron gallop

911 are you
getting all this
from long before
and likely after

Please wait
I'm going to patch you
~~*up*~~ *through, don't hang* ~~*up*~~
out with those men, simple, easy,
as it were
the unfinished wheel

who do you blame when the tunnel opens
when he steps forward again
it is not the first time

is it you now
the air mute   grievous
do you play the animal
disobeying   yielding to the floor

VERMILION

Avalanche lilies dotted the snowmelt
the night I lost my keys. It grew
difficult to speak, to undo the last hour,
his body on a bender again,
bones a thirsty loam. Midnight. Still early.
The next neon sign torches
a vermilion night. He goads me to run
into the swollen road, every ending
touchable twin pinpricks of light
ready to deface me—
cold freedom, black highway, this way this way, this
time double lines divide the unpredictable
into before and after.
I'm certain if I stop I'll be safe,
levelled but alive on a hospital bed.
I can tell them how I wanted this
night to end,
sleepwalking dunes in dusk,
singing barn owls to sleep,
the moon nowhere to be seen—
the brightening dream, only a flame
where his head should be.

THEREFORE

The lion stitched from his mouth. I came to, my name the longest bridge. Therefore: blindness, the ethanol dare. I cut my shade. His throat holds *soon* to *bitters*. Summer running upward. His unbroken musk. Render its beauty as other—the yellow light shakes his hand into fire. Therefore, consequence, his glass edges, the fracture, doctor inconsolable. You can't stop neon under the door. Therefore. Oronoco, matusalem platino, his last pour before blackout, the lightning, old boat gifted in the early hours. Therefore his apologies, the dirt turned. I'm used to being sidelined—therefore,

SOFT STALKER

the worst thing is the cop doesn't ask   about the worst time
but the first time

the time it took for my ex to follow   snap   call   call again   private phone number
        four five one
slow air when I answered   when the call sounded its end

I cannot prove the last caller   was the last man to grip my wrists
I cannot prove my level of fear

:: are you drinking your fear ::
        :: hiding your fear ::
                :: breathing your fear ::
                        :: plotting your fear ::

(don't make this
about me.
every cop in this chop shop
makes it about me)

I learned to track by sound
more often than somewhere   the distance blown sideways

Walgreens parking lot flooded in light
        what a night to hide   under metal bodies echoing
                what he returned to

when he screamed my name
I went blind

there will never be an end   only after
                and after

the cop labels this phase *soft stalking*
label   sticker   sticky   sticky   notefolder
between SIN
        for "since the law is soft you must protect yourself"
and SON
        for "sonless wonder the law reaps itself for the pure"

examples: soft cobweb text quick vid solo video
example pic: heady selfie strut down the street hashtag singlelife
example vid: a rope in a tree is it /
a toy or my future is it /
a swing or a sentence /
for boys like me

snapchat handle new friend request
snapchat handle new friend request
snapchat handle new friend request

for months my phone buzz kept me numb
I learned to sit on my hands
scolded child

silence for weeks like a black wind ripped through town
next morning an old friend texts *hey you who's this dude*   *says he knows you*   *wants to meet me*
to talk   *about you*

our cells hibernate in a room with no air
architect of our actions we adapt to   slow chords of discontent

vertigo in the cubicle
the water glass   the table   the fluorescent ceiling

the cop   never asks   about the complexities of male::male relationships
the cop   blinks twice   each time I say *ex-boyfriend*
the cop   tosses out   the word *affinity*

and I sink into my forest of animalself—

I armadillo below a sparking lake
I hummingbird the furthest nectar
I mayfly under enormous ferns   for the singular dance   the 24-hour lifespan

THE TUNNEL

he can't keep your eyes
looking backward all the time

the dark fighting light under your eyelids
pulls you close to what you cannot see

it's in your best interest to mistrust
the ones who watch you watch

onlookers on the train in the reflection
the shifter shuffling in the corner

someone stays hidden under a hood
from everyone else's eyes

someone enters the train
someone steps off

is it him, murky in the reflection
his hands still full of fire

someone opens an emergency window
and the steel screams

into the tunnel, the dark
quietly congratulating itself

in every corner of the train
there is something there

where
there

where the head should be
in the dark it's a giant

red light and it's blinking
the deeper we go

TILT

I dream of his return, not long after
red and blue lights painted the peace
of my apartment's white walls,
the spring wind passing as a tunnel

under the locked door, the nights
I considered all the ways to seal it.
My pockets were weighted with spare keys.
I wrapped my sprained wrist in tensor

to hide the bruises where his hands
held me down. I stripped the bedsheets
to rid the room of his familiar odour,
cast spells in bursts of eucalyptus mist,

emerged weeks later, begrudging the early bloom,
dragonflies and diamonds dancing
on the lake, sky a lavender blush,
my body warm on the cedarwood

but fearing the dream, a step back,
the fire still burning in his hands
whose end is not the end
but the inevitable tilt.

THE MAYFLY

Some mornings you come out of it
dawned and hollow as the fists thrown by ghosts
at sunrise. REM sleep never seems to hit until morning.

Another late one, cresting the slope of a scree
from his nightly violence. Gravol to quell the queer
feelings. Don't panic it's just another night terror

another face in the dark, think thoughts happy happy
life a continuum rubber band the year I lived
his fire measured between handspans here to here.

It's the booze before bed—that's what beckons them.
Yellow dog beer, cider out of left field, hoofprint
gin under a silent sky eclipsing the lanterns.

You are what you eat. Often I go hungry
before bed for that fervid pinch in my ribs,
acid's sting behind my tongue.

Of all the creatures on Earth,
which one would you pick
to be free of your fear?

MAKE GOOD

How do you intend

It to end the road its roar

To nowhere the habitual

Leaving we revisit once

A long age thaws

Solid in our forgetting

Did you return

To make good

On your boyhood instinct,

Playing animal, uncanny

The southern blur

At the train's terminal gate

How does it begin

I know not

To listen to the city

Braided in light

The second step

A heavy familiar

How much time

Before I guess

Myself back

Into that world

Saying

I am not

Afraid–

You first

I

II

III

IV

V

THE CALLING

At first the world was body.
I didn't question the gold
hardening its rivers inside me.

Boy on the phone for you, my sister cooed.
He asked to meet behind the pool
and I heard my name ripple in the wind.

I had no map for this part of town,
only my known, strange derivatives stirring.
Streetlights converged to a single pin

as stars crept from my eyes.
Sheer ribbon of night,
I tripped on its edge.

We weren't convinced of the danger
after so much hugger-mugger at school,
admonition lingering low as a cloud.

Blond wind susurrus I watched him
lean his bike under a motion light.
My insides chimed their separate lakes.

A tinge of chlorine stung my nose.
He caught me in the handlebar's mirror
concentric with the moon, a silver shim,

and we stood for a time, trembling.
I saw into his world and he saw mine,
both of us woozy in our reverie.

FULLBLOWN

blond wind susurrus
mimic I hear you

air throws its dusk and I colour sepia
along the unlit road—

barefoot razed field
colts gambol geese V and echo

far from the wreck room shivoo
my insides chime their separate lakes

fullblown ache in summer the girl on TV
cries to the girl on TV
my brother blows up pixelated cities on TV
I am not on TV I am not
but I want to

tumble the golden droke
sky a vermilion scythe I am not a girl but I want to

fullblown the boy in red shorts
opens a window a space in my chest

is this what they call *out of body*
falling inward and splitting my own rope

tomorrow's fear is tomorrow's face of my body

my body thistles in my devil in red shorts and climbing

black walnut trunk without words
blond wind susurrus mimic I hear you

drumming down
balloon and blow away

boy above boy below boy above boy
below boy above boy below boy above

it's impossible not to cross hot tar
and think *this is heaven, all this burning*

FISSION

Another word for love eludes me.
I'm thinking of the man
with his name
in coloured lights
on the wall.
Enter the door
and be filled with newness.
We've stopped talking
but the nights continue.
It's what we do,
a series of firsts. When at last
we exhaust the afterward,
the body's fusion,
we split in two.
Tomorrow I'll say my name
to a stranger for the first time.
His hair will be blond and soft
and my face will hurt
from too much smiling.
I'll know this man because I've loved them all.

MEANWHILE

What about the time I shattered
a row of basement windows, cruising

my two-wheeler coaster downhill
after busting out his bedroom door,

my underwear nowhere and my head
a deadstare pumpkin brimming in night air.

He was home alone. I was twelve. I came
to unfurl the leaves hardening inside me.

I kissed like they do on TV, feigning aplomb,
thinking *this is what a teenage boy desires.*

The tunnel began to form and I crawled
into the sky. How wide the ambit.

In the parking lot the older kids killed it
with their stories, their names, their viridity.

Miles away, a boy dove into a river of gold,
his body flexuous, extant under the sun.

NOTES

The epigraph is taken from Elizabeth Willis's "The Human Abstract," *Alive: New and Selected Poems*, 2015, NYRB Poets. Used with permission.

The recurring motif of red lights is inspired by Jewel Kilcher's song "Barcelona."

The community centre in "Ravine" and the creek in "The Big Dark" are both located at Renfrew Community Park in East Vancouver.

The dashes in "Watergun" recreate Emily Dickinson's poetic style.

"Strawberry Island" was the name given by my older siblings to a wooded area in Point Roberts, Washington.

"Someday You Will Ache" recalls a game my younger sister and I played as kids—we would lie in the middle of our street and wait for cars to approach.

The black dogs in "Afloat" are English folkloric omens of danger and death.

In "As If," The Wanderer is the name of a rundown bar in *Shadowrun*, a Sega Genesis video game.

The style of questioning in "A Violence" is inspired by W.S. Merwin's poem, "What Is Modern" from *Opening the Hand*, 1983, Antheneum.

Lines in "The Tunnel" are inspired by Vasko Popa's poem, "Hide-and-Seek" from *Selected Poems*, translated by Charles Simic, 2019, NYRB Poets.

The pool in "The Calling" is a wading pool at Slocan Park in East Vancouver.

ACKNOWLEDGEMENTS

To the staff at University of Alberta Press: Michelle Lobkowicz, the jurors, and everyone else who believed in my work. Thank you for making my first full-length collection a reality.

To Natalie Olsen for designing the perfect cover art.

To Annick MacAskill, who edited my manuscript and helped turn it into this book. Endless thanks and gratitude for your poetic wisdom.

To family and friends who have cheered for my poetry over the years.

To Jim Johnstone at Anstruther Press, who published my first chapbook, *Dastardly*, containing these poems: "As You Were," "Dastardly," "It's Like That, Is It," "Nick the Dick," "Someday You Will Ache," and "The Floor Was Water."

To James Hawes at Turret House Press, who published my second chapbook, *a blurred wind swirls back for you*. A previous version of section III is published here as "switchrail" and "Vermilion."

Gratitude to the editors of literary magazines where early versions of the following poems appeared:

In *CV2*: "Touch Anywhere to Begin" (Volume 43.2), "Student Debt" (Volume 38.1).

In *EVENT*: "The First" and "Traffic Light" (Issue 50.3).

In *The Ex-Puritan*: "Make Good" (Issue 57).

In *The Fiddlehead*: "Meanwhile" and "Someday You Will Ache" (Issue 289).

In *Grain*: "The Dark Gap" (Volume 47.4).

In *The Malahat Review*: "The Calling," "fullblown," and "soft stalker" (Issue 221); "Dastardly," "The Circuit," and "Afloat" (Issue 217); "A Violence" (Issue 210).

In *Pinhole Poetry*: "Fission" (Issue 1.3).

In *Prairie Fire*: "The Big Dark" (Volume 42.2). Selected for inclusion in *Best Canadian Poetry 2023*.

In *Train : a poetry journal*: "Heatwave" and "The Tunnel" (Summer 2020).